Celebrating Forgiveness
An original text
drafted by Michael Vasey

by
Trevor Lloyd
Former Archdeacon of Barnstaple,
member of the Liturgical Commission 1981-2002

Phillip Tovey
Director of Reader Training, Diocese of Oxford

GROVE BOOKS LIMITED
RIDLEY HALL RD CAMBRIDGE CB3 9HU

Contents

THE COVER PICTURE
is a fictional sample of appropriate newspaper headlines

First Impression December 2004
ISSN 0951-2667
ISBN 1 85174 581 5

Preface

This Liturgical Study is dedicated to the memory of Michael Vasey, liturgy tutor at St John's College, Durham (1975-1998), and a member of the Church of England's Liturgical Commission (1985-1998), who died in June 1998. It reproduces the text which he originally drafted for the Commission in the early 1990s, as amended both by the Commission and by the House of Bishops, on which discussion was effectively suspended in 1995. At that stage the Commission proposed to further the discussion on penitence and reconciliation in the church by publishing its proposed texts together with some background essays, but the project, which Michael was to have edited, was halted by his untimely death.

We are grateful to Canon Gordon Oliver, Bishop's Officer for Ministry and Training in the Diocese of Rochester, and Revd Dr Gordon Jeanes, then a member of the Commission's working group on reconciliation and Sub-Warden of St Michael's College Llandaff, now Vicar of St Anne's, Wandsworth, for permission to reprint edited versions of papers they wrote to help the Liturgical Commission in its original thinking about this subject, and to Canon Professor Oliver O'Donovan, Regius Professor of Moral Theology at Oxford, for permission to quote from his lecture on the occasion of the twentieth anniversary of Grove Books in 1992, which provided some of the stimulus for Michael Vasey's work on this. The lecture, and Michael's response, were published as *Liturgy and Ethics* (Grove Ethics Series no 89, 1993). We are also grateful to Revd Mark Earey, Michael's literary executor, and to the Library at Sarum College, Salisbury, where Michael's papers are held, for their help in finding and permission to quote from his unpublished correspondence and notes. The footnotes to the liturgical text indicate Michael Vasey's own description of his souces and are mostly in his own words.

1
Reconciliation: Michael Vasey's Work Considered

by David Stancliffe (Chairman of the Liturgical Commission)

When the Common Worship texts for *Rites on the Way and Reconciliation and Restoration* were published as GS 1546 for consideration by the General Synod in July 2004, two short paragraphs at the end of the introduction acknowledged the debt of the Liturgical Commission to Michael Vasey, our erstwhile colleague.

Michael had been responsible not only for much of the initial drafting, but for keeping before us the continuing problem of post-baptismal sin. How was it that the redeemed, baptised into the death and resurrection of Christ, could slip from that glorious inheritance; and if they did – as we all do –, how could they be reclaimed for Christ?

The reality of this predicament was taken seriously by Michael, and it emerged in his work in two ways. First, as we worked on the initiation rites, Michael became convinced that the rites needed a staged approach, so that candidates who were approaching the sacraments could celebrate the stages of their growing into belonging and believing; and second, that at the other side of the celebration of baptism itself, we needed a form of reconciliation and restoration that set individual sin and penitence in a context that was ecclesial and social, as well as personal.

These theological convictions drove Michael's thinking for much of his last years, and his drafting has been immensely significant for our common life and worship in this area. He was the drafter of the Report *On the Way*, which emerged from discussions between the Board of Education, the Board of Mission and the Liturgical Commission. We held a residential meeting, the first we supposed of a long series of such, and found within hours that we were of a common mind. *On the Way* provided the church with a vision of a total process of coming to faith, of experiencing the pattern of belonging and believing, of formation, and of conversion as a process which might continue through the celebration of the sacraments and result in a pattern of living.

Michael's place in the Commission's sub-group on the Initiation Rites and his work on the Steering Committee of the Synod's long-running Revision Committee were the most visible public expressions of his work in this area, but we had long agreed that when the full volume of the Common Worship initiation services was finally drawn together, the service of baptism and confirmation would need to be complemented by what has now emerged as *Rites on the Way* and as *Reconciliation and Restoration*.

Now that the Commission has produced the drafts for this material in GS 1546, which were the subject of a debate in the General Synod in July 2004 and are being revised by the Commission before being commended by the House of Bishops, the work in this area of which Michael was the prime drafter is seeing the light of day in an official form. This makes the publication of the original papers and of Michael's notes on them a matter of considerable interest. While it was judged prudent in the 1990s to let the interplay of the new initiation rites, new catechetical material and the admission of the baptized to communion form the church's mind on just what might be needed in *Rites on the Way*, there was also considerable reluctance at that stage to proceed with services of *Reconciliation and Restoration*: the Commission had been advised that they would be held to be an alternative to the Visitation of the Sick in the Book of Common Prayer, and thus subject to the full liturgical authorization processes in the Synod. But with the publication of the services for Wholeness and Healing in *Common Worship: Pastoral Services*, and the assurance that the proposed services for Reconciliation and Restoration would contain only authorized absolutions, there came a renewed impetus to draw together what might precede the central core of the initiation rites and what needed to follow it in a Common Worship volume that claimed to provide for the whole range of celebrations around baptism.

What this Alcuin/GROW Study does is to place this additional material in its theological context. Over the years that I have been associated with it, the Liturgical Commission has been the arena where I have experienced the best and most consistently invigorating theological discussions. Focussed by the need to produce a rite for worship that the whole church would use, and conscious that the doctrine of the Church of England is to a major extent both defined and taught by its worship, the Commission spends a good deal of its time in full session in theological debate and discussion. These papers and Michael Vasey's drafts and theological reflections that form the core of this book will be of great interest not only to historians of the rites as they have developed but to those practitioners who are clamouring to use the rites as they work their patient way through the processes which lead to commendation and publication.

+David Sarum
All Saints-tide 2004

2
The Text Explained
by the Editors, Trevor Lloyd and Phillip Tovey

While the text of the draft Church of England reconciliation rites was only comprehensively committed to paper by Michael Vasey in the early months of 1994, Michael had been involved in discussion of the idea and possibilities for some years.[1] In January 1992 the twentieth anniversary of Grove Books was celebrated by an event at which the main speaker was Professor Oliver O'Donovan, Regius Professor of Moral Theology in the University of Oxford. The title of the lecture was 'Liturgy and Ethics' and his concluding remarks were on liturgy and penance.

'Let me say something in conclusion that takes us a little further. A work that liturgy can do, which is fundamental to any Christian exercise of moral thought or moral teaching, is pronouncing forgiveness.

'It is the very heart of the gospel that we are free to act only as we are forgiven and accept forgiveness; and if the church intends to take seriously the ordering of its moral commitments in a world where all is moral confusion, it must surely do so by declaring and claiming God's forgiveness; Otherwise the church will either be a moralizing, Pelagian church, or else afraid ever to proclaim its moral commitments out of sheer fear of Pelagianism, in which case it will have only an inward, mystical gospel.

'Paul Ramsey draws our attention to a liturgical example that he found helpful, and that was the Orthodox liturgy for the second marriage of the divorced.[2] He found this an excellent model of how, by pronouncing forgiveness, the church could both illuminate and teach the moral structure that surrounded marriage. I would like to take this thought further, and repeat a suggestion that I made some years ago that we need a service of the public reconciliation of the penitent.

'This could be the key that opened the locked door of our difficulties with "scandal" in the church: not only the place of divorced and remarried people in the church, but the place of homosexuals in the church, the place of capitalists in the church, the place of everything that gives scandal and affront. Private confession has achieved much, no doubt, over the centuries. It has not achieved this, which is to articulate the church's public moral commitment, and to make the church at ease with its own members, who are, all of them, sinners in one way or another and some of them notorious sinners.

'Imagine something like this: by New Year's Day candidates will apply to the bishop requesting to be admitted to the annual service of reconciliation. They will make a private statement of what it is they have done of which

---

1   For Michael's wider interests in liturgy including reconciliation see Colin Buchanan (ed.), *Michael Vasey—Liturgist and Friend* (Grove Books Ltd, 1999).
2   *Principles in the Public Realm* (OUP, 1982).

6

they are ashamed. This will be accompanied by a letter from the parish priest or equivalent pastor, who will give details of the counselling and pastoral care that have been given, and will indicate his or her view of whether the candidate displays a well-judged self-understanding penitence. Perhaps also a letter from a close associate or friend who will vouch for the account given of the circumstances, so that nothing material or important is left out. Applications will then be screened to weed out the exhibitionists, habituees, and over-tender consciences, and perhaps in some cases to recommend the candidate to have a year's more counselling.

'Then, at the beginning of Lent, permission is given to the successful candidates, who will be asked thereupon to abstain from communion for the season, and will be invited to attend a service in the cathedral on Holy Saturday. At the service the names of the candidates will be read out and there will be a brief statement, agreed by the candidate and the bishop, about what the repentance is for — enough to make the thing not an empty gesture, but not enough to excite prurient curiosity. For example:

> "Michael Jones acknowledges before the people of God that he has been unfaithful to his wife, and asks God's forgiveness and the prayers of the community, that he may be strengthened to serve God in holiness from this day forward."

> "Penny Smith acknowledges before the people of God that she has been dishonest in her business dealings, and unfeeling to those who have worked with her as employees. She asks for God's forgiveness and the prayers of the community . . ."[3] and so on.

'Whereupon the bishop will invite the congregation to affirm their welcome to these penitents, and, the congregation having declared that it will, he will pronounce forgiveness and lay hands on each in prayer.

'Scandal is a problem of the public earthly existence of the church, an earthly existence which fails to refer in that "formed" way to the work of God and seems discordant with it. Scandal is the public dissonance of the church's common life with the the work and the grace of God, and it can only be dealt with by public acts. But the true public act of the church is an act of liturgy. We have our other public forms of the church: we have place of everything that gives scandal parliaments and we have councils, and they serve us well enough, but we do not see the *esse* of the church in them. We see the esse of the church in its liturgy, where, brought to unanimity of mind and clarity of purpose, the church makes its formed reference together to the work of God to which it responds. That is why theological moralists may sometimes dare to express themselves in liturgical forms, without, I hope, appearing too intrusive to those whose terrain it is, just as it has long been understood that dogmatic theologians may express themselves in liturgical forms too.'

3   Cf the text below, p.15

His lecture was published as *Liturgy and Ethics* (Grove Ethics Series No 89) with a response by Michael Vasey who reminded us that, when Oliver addressed this theme in his inaugural lecture, he mentioned as possible candidates 'indifferent parents who were learning to get along with their children' and 'theologians who had seen the error of romantic idealistic theology!' Michael's comment was:

'Such a rite would make visible the Church's commitment to both forgiveness and moral reality. It would also illuminate modern controversy about absolution. So-called "sacramental confession" is a conflation of spiritual direction and ecclesiastical discipline. A public rite of reconciliation would help Anglicans to see the difference between official, charismatic (prophetic), and liturgical absolution.

'His [i.e.O'Donovan's] proposals for this rite have, of course, a very substantial history in the Church's tradition. They follow closely the practice set out so vividly in the Didascalia.[4] For a model liturgical text one might turn to the early Roman rite which places near the start of the Maundy Thursday liturgy a finely crafted petition for acceptance by the archdeacon ("Venerable Bishop, the moment of grace has come. . .") followed shortly after by the bishop leading the penitents in a sort of liturgical conga through the assembly while he sings of the joy of the angels over sinners who repent.'

Another influence on Michael's thinking was the 11th International Congress of Societas Liturgica on 'Penance in Contemporary Scholarship'. This enabled him to keep an ongoing discussion with Roman Catholics. Michael had particular interest in the attempts to develop an order of penitents.[5] He was also interested in the connections between such an order and other approaches particularly in the steps of Alcoholics Anonymous. All this contributed to the background of his thinking.

When the Liturgical Commission set up a sub-group[6] to consider the subject of initiation[7], and within that to look again at reconciliation, it was natural for Michael to take the lead and to put these principles into effect as he began to draft the text. His own explanation of the four rites which emerged early in 1994 is clear both about the sources for his ideas (and some of his texts) and also about the primary place of the diocesan rite, the existence of which is the context which makes the other rites possible.[8]

---

4   Sebastian Brock and Michael Vasey (eds.) *The Liturgical Portions of the Didascalia* (Grove Liturgical Studies no 29, Grove Books, 1982). For a careful discussion of the practice there described, see Kari Rahner, *Theological Investigations vol XV* (Crossroad, NY, 1982) pp.225ff.
5   E.g. R.J.Kennedy, *Reconciliation: The Continuing Agenda* (Pastoral Press, Washington, 1987).
6   The members of this sub-group included David Stancliffe, Kenneth Stevenson, Pat Harris, John Sweet, and Gordon Jeanes.
7   'Official restoration of sinners needs to be related to baptism and the Holy Spirit—the primary referent of John 20.23' Michael had written in correspondence with Geoffrey Rowell in *News of Liturgy* in 1988.
8   In the same letter he wrote 'I believe there is a case for restoring a public rite of restoration of sinners to make visible, in a phrase of David Silk, "the scandal of forgiveness". Needed in its own right, it would set other forms of declaration of forgiveness in a better context.'

'The diocesan rite has as its main inspirations: the ancient pattern as set out, for example, in the Didascalia and in Rahner's reading of the same[9]; the proposals of Oliver O'Donovan for a public diocesan rite as set out in the recent Grove Ethical Study *Ethics and Liturgy* as well as in his earlier writing; the public rite of the Gelasian Sacramentary.

'In framing the parish rite I took as my mental example a treasurer who had absconded with parish funds! It tries to take seriously both the congregational dimension of Anglican church life and the episcopal order in which such life is set. You will see that it looks less drastically to the Gelasian texts (and the diocesan rite) and more to the familiar patterns of the parish communion.

'The two individual rites attempt to follow the example of the USA Book of Common Prayer in having two rites, one Western and one Eastern. In the case of the Western rite I took as my starting point various ACS leaflets etc.[10] and also the text and revision committee report of the abortive synodical attempt to produce a rite in 1981/3. Form Two is based on the second USA form and its underlying Orthodox model while attempting to find more adequate liturgical language. In both cases I have attempted to find brevity and flow, to respect current practice, and also to bring out the link. between reconciliation and baptism.'

'Our hope is that the context of baptism and public reconciliation will make the place of the individual rites clear and acceptable to a wide range of Anglican opinion. In the light of the heat of past controversies there are two aspects of these individual rites that it may be helpful to spell out further.

1   the opening notes make careful reference to the 1552/1662 exhortation and indicate very clearly that these rites are not more than possible forms. One aim here is to take seriously the issues that Colin Buchanan raises about the interpretation of the 1662 exhortation and its differences from 1549. A second is to counter his objection that it is unnecessary and restrictive to authorize a rite given the legitimate breadth of practice implied in the Canon Law.

2   the second area is the question of the form of the absolution. Our situation here is helped by the fact that A Service of the Word gave official authorization to a number of absolution texts. In the two individual forms we give two forms of absolution preceded by the rubric. This, of course, has the effect—among other things—of allowing the BCP form. The first absolution in Form One derives from the Scottish Episcopal Church and was authorized with *A Service of the Word*. The other three forms will require authorizing if they are to share the status of other absolutions. The second absolution in Form One attempts to provide a modern and acceptable form of an "Ego te absolvo" formula. It is the subject of Gordon Jeanes' papers.[11] Important

9   See footnote 4 above.
10   Additional Curates' Society.
11   See 'Absolution Reconsidered', an edited version of these papers by Gordon Jeanes, below p 41.

from my point of view is the dynamic treatment of the Spirit and the dimension of release from the experienced grip of sin. The first absolution in Form Two has its inspiration in an Orthodox text and a prayer in the USA BCP. The second absolution in Form Two comes from *Lent, Holy Week, Easter*—and has not, as far as I can see, moved from commended to authorized status.

'In the case of the diocesan rite there are various prayers, which contribute to the process of absolution and have their origin in various Eastern and Western prayers. In my mind this forms a commentary on what constitutes absolution.'

The examination of this text inevitably invites comparison with the texts seen by the General Synod in July 2004 and commended by the House of Bishops under the title *Reconciliation and Restoration* (GS1546). These newly commended rites do not include a diocesan rite. It was clear in 1994-5 that this part of the draft would have to be withdrawn if it was to be approved by the House of Bishops for sending to Synod, despite the thoroughly researched historical antecedents for such a rite (see Gordon Jeanes' essay later).[12] The bishops were particularly concerned not to do anything which might give rise to comment in the media, though more than one bishop said how useful it would be to have such a rite, if not authorized and in the public domain, at least in a file in the study for use if needed. None of this text now survives in the new provision.

One of the elements in this text is the care taken over the individual penitent, focussed on the enrolment service, preceded by counselling and pastoral care. This brief service, which might be a part of another public service, follows the pattern of Michael Vasey's other *On the Way* drafts, of marking in a liturgical and public way some spiritual commitment to begin a process, to embark on the journey, the goal of which is set out in the rite.

In the newly commended services the parish rite is also very different from the text we have here, focussing on 'prayer and penitence' where this original draft has a section on 'the celebration of forgiveness' which focuses on an individual or group of people, providing opportunities for public confession and forgiveness. The new rite is far more general in nature, and could easily be a general penitential rite rather than one focussed on the need for forgiveness for individuals, though it does allow for the ministry of prayer for individuals and the laying on of hands for the ministry of healing. The rich formulae for absolution and the prayer for the laying on of hands have gone, as has the specially crafted eucharistic preface. But all is not lost. Quite apart from the seminal contribution of Michael's rite, the fact that the 2004 rites are commended and not authorized means much of this text may still be used where circumstances are appropriate.

---

12   In June 1994 some members of the Commission expressed reservation at the inclusion of a rite of public reconciliation, while others supported it as the norm from which the rationale for individual rites of reconciliation derived. The Commission concluded 'There were circumstances in which the use of such a public rite was appropriate, but the dangers of uncontrolled use giving rise to a judgemental and narrow ecclesiology were recognized'.

3
Reconciliation and Restoration: the Text
(Drafted by Michael Vasey)

(a) INTRODUCTORY NOTE

In Baptism Christians are called by God to forsake a way of life characterized by sin and death and to enter into the new order of right living that has been ocreated through the resurrection of Jesus Christ. 'We have been buried with him by baptism into death, so that, as Christ was raised from the dead by the glory of the Father, we too might walk in newness of life...So you must consider yourself dead to sin and alive to God in Christ Jesus' (Romans 6.4-11).

The Church lives in a tension between the new order made possible in Christ and the continuing reality of human sin. The First Letter of John says both, 'No one born of God commits sin' (3.9) and also, 'If we say we have no sin we deceive ourselves' (1.8). In baptism God proclaims to the individual and to the Church the final triumph of the new creation in the face of this pervasive reality of the rebellion, disorder and alienation of human sinfulness. Many aspects of the Church's life are deeply affected by her continuing struggle against sin. In every area of the Church's life the grace of God is at work drawing Christians from the darkness of sin to the new light of Christ.

Healing is one of the images used in scripture for the restoring and reconciling of those whose lives have been marred by sin. In many of the healing miracles in the Gospels the Greek word *sozo* (= save, heal) is used to indicate both physical healing and the deeper reconcilation brought by Christ. The figure of the suffering servant of Isaiah 52.13—53.12 foreshadows both Jesus' costly ministry of healing (Matthew 8.17) and also his redemptive bearing of human sin. 'By his wounds we have been healed' (1 Peter 2.24). Many Christians see healing services as occasions to seek prayer about sin and disorder in their lives.

The New Testament urges Christians, 'Confess your sins to one another, and pray for another that you may be healed' (James 5.16). This exhortation finds its primary fulfilment as Christians join together in a common life of discipleship. The experience of giving and receiving forgiveness is integral to the life of any Christian fellowship. However in the lives of individual Christians and of Christian communities there are particular moments when the reality of human sin needs to be faced, when the wounds inflicted by sin need to be healed, and the wonderful gift of forgiveness received and celebrated afresh.

The Church's role in ministering forgiveness to individuals is taught in scripture (cf John 20.19-23, Acts 2.38). This authority finds its primary expression in the administration of baptism. It also underlies the Church's response to serious and public sin in the lives of baptized people (Matt 18.15-20, 1 Cor 5.1-5, 2 Cor 2.5-11, 1 Tim 5.20). In exercising this authority the Church depends on the presence and discernment of the Holy Spirit; great care needs to be taken to express the gentleness and patience of Christ (Matt 11.25-30, 12.12-21, 18.10-14).

The Church must never attempt to use this authority as a way of gaining power over or manipulating individuals.

The forms of service in this section are intended to meet some of the situations in which the Church confronts the fact of human weakness and sin and appropriates again the new life proclaimed in baptism.[13]

The Diocesan Rite, may be used in the case of sins that have been a source of public scandal or have done grievous damage to the health and witness of the Christian fellowship. The aim of the service is to celebrate the love and mercy of God and not to glamorize the sin or the sinner.

The Parish Rite may appropriately be used where serious and public sin, either individual or corporate, has done grievous damage to the health and witness of a congregation, or where members of the congregation have been in open hostility with each other.

The Forms for Individual Reconciliation, may appropriately be used when a person's conscience is burdened with a particular sin, when a person wishes to make a new beginning in the Christian life, or as part of a regular personal discipline.

(b) DIOCESAN RITE OF RECONCILIATION[14]

INTRODUCTORY NOTES
1. This order may be used in the case of sins that have been a source of public scandal or have done grievous damage to the health and witness of the Christian fellowship. The aim of the service is to celebrate the love and mercy of God and not to glamorize the sin or the sinner.
2. This service will only be used with the agreement of the bishop and the presiding minister will be the bishop or a priest appointed by him. It would be appropriate if one such service was held each year in the cathedral at the end of Lent, possibly on the Saturday before Palm Sunday or on Maundy Thursday before the Eucharist of the Last Supper. Public notice should be given of such a service. It is not necessary that the style of the service should be grand or formal.
3. It is envisaged that those designated as penitents in this rite would have received counselling and pastoral care before being enrolled as such. Before allowing a person to be enrolled as a penitent, the bishop or person appointed by him should receive statements from the person and from a priest with pastoral responsibility for them, stating the nature of the sin and the nature of the counselling and pastoral care being pursued. The priest should also indicate whether the person is showing appropriate signs of true repentance. It may be appropriate for a friend also to be designated as the penitent's companion. This order shall not be used until every effort has been made to put right what has gone wrong and there is good reason to believe that those concerned are established in a stable way of life.
4. Where a person is to be enrolled as a penitent they may use Sections Introduction and Confession and Counsel from one of the Forms for Individual Reconciliation [pages 24-29] in confessing their sins to a priest. They may be publicly admitted as a penitent using the form indicated below; this could be done on Ash Wednesday or at any appropriate service. One of the ways this period of penitence may be marked is to abstain from receiving Holy Communion for an agreed period before this service is celebrated.

---

13 Apart from the three paragraphs on the individual rites which follow, this Introduction written in March-April 1994 by Michael Vasey, stands unchanged as the 'Theological Introduction' to the recently commended (2004) 'Reconciliation and Restoration' rites.
14 MV's original title was 'A Celebration of Forgiveness and Reconciliation'. As he said, 'I have tried to follow the basic approach to structure of [the] Celebration of Healing and Wholeness'.

5   The content of the confession made shall under no circumstances be disclosed to anyone without the consent of the penitent and the agreement of the bishop. Where appropriate, a form of words may be agreed and used at Section 10 in the rite. Such a statement should not go beyond a brief and general statement of the matter concerned.

6. This rite is normally celebrated within the Eucharist. But if a major liturgical rite of the day—eg. Maundy Thursday or Holy Saturday—is to follow, then a Ministry of the Word with the Rite of Reconciliation may be sufficient.

7. Hymns, chants or songs may be used at appropriate positions in the rite.

ENROLMENT AS A PENITENT

(This order may be used in public worship)

After the Prayers of intercession in the Eucharist the priest says,

Brothers and sisters in Christ, none of us is righteous of ourselves, and all of us need the forgiveness which Christ has made available to us through his death and resurrection. Jesus did not come to condemn the world but that the world might be saved through him. In the face of sin we are not to despair but to embrace the love and forgiveness which God has pledged to us in our baptism.

The gospels give us many examples of God's mercy to those who come to him in repentance and faith. Today our *brother/sister* N seeks our prayer and support as *he/she* enrols as a penitent. *He/she* is conscious of the seriousness of sin and is seeking God's grace to make a new start in the *Christian* way. On ____ in the Cathedral *he/she* will join with the church in a celebration of the forgiveness and reconciliation which are ours in Jesus Christ.

During this period of repentance and reflection *he/she* needs the love of his fellow Christians. Will you support *him/her* with your love and prayers?

All   **We will**

Let us now pray in silence

Silence is kept

The priest may lay hands on the person and says

Gentle and gracious God[15],
you seek and save those who have gone astray:
we pray for our *brother/sister* N.
Grant *him/her* a true understanding of *him/herself*
grace to amend *his/her* life, and faith in your restoring and healing love.
May *he/she* be to us an example of repentance
and a sign of joy and hope
within the love of Jesus Christ our Lord. **Amen.**

---

15   The Liturgical Commission registered its strong preference for the original opening phrase. The House of Bishops' Theological Group wanted 'Gentle and' omitted.

PUBLIC CELEBRATION OF FORGIVENESS AND RECONCILIATION

THE PREPARATION

1. *During the gathering of the assembly and the entrance of the ministers, psalms, hymns or chants may be sung. The penitents are seated toward the back of the Church with an agreed companion.*

2. *THE GREETING*

    In the name of Christ
    who was wounded for our sins
    and lives to bring us freedom
    we welcome you:
    Grace and peace be with you
    And also with you.

3. God was in Christ, reconciling the world to himself
    not counting our sins against us.

    God made him to be sin who was without sin
    that we might receive[16] the righteousness of God.

    God makes this appeal to us:
    be reconciled to God.

    Behold, now is the acceptable time.
    Now is the day of salvation.

4. *THE COLLECT*

    Grant, Lord,
    that we who are baptized into the death
    of your Son our Saviour Jesus Christ
    may continually put to death our evil desires
    and be buried with him;
    that through the grave and gate of death
    we may pass to our joyful resurrection;
    through his merits, who died and was buried and rose again for us,
    your Son, Jesus Christ our Lord. **Amen.**[17]

---

16 Originally 'that we might know'; 'share' and embrace' were also considered.
17 ASB, Easter Eve.

THE MINISTRY OF THE WORD

5.　　*THE OLD TESTAMENT READING*[18]

6.　　*A psalm or canticle may be sung*

7.　　*THE NEW TESTAMENT READING*

8.　　*A hymn or canticle may be sung*

9.　　*THE GOSPEL*

THE RECONCILIATION

10.　　*A priest stands with the penitent towards the back of the church. The Bishop stands before the assembly.*

The day of God's mercy and our salvation is here, for now is the acceptable time.[19] The Good Shepherd has laid down his life for his sheep. The servant has given his life as a ransom for many. God sprinkles clean water over us and pours his Spirit upon us.
People of God, these our brothers and sisters come before us as those who acknowledge their sin and seek with us the grace and forgiveness that are in Jesus Christ.

The names of the penitent are read at this point and, where agreed by the Bishop, a brief statement may be included about the matter of which they are repenting. Words such as the following may be used. They may be spoken by a priest or a companion chosen by the penitent.

N acknowledges before the people of God that *he/she* has fallen into sin *[or a particular matter may be mentioned]* and asks God's forgiveness and the prayers of the community that *he/she* may walk in newness of life.[20]

11.　　*The Bishop says*

Since we all sin and fall short of the glory of God,
let us kneel in silence and pray for the grace and forgiveness of God.

Silence is kept

18　The readings set out in the table at the end were originally specified here in the text.
19　This sentence was changed because of doubts expressed by the House of Bishops Theological Group in September 1994 about the original, which was from the Gelasian Sacramentary: 'The moment of grace has come; the day of God's mercy and salvation is here.'
20　After Oliver O'Donovan in *Ethics and Liturgy* (see pp 6-7 above)

Let us confess our sins to almighty God
Holy and loving God,
from dust you have formed us in your likeness,
and redeemed us from death by your cross;
by water and Spirit
you have washed away our sins,
clothed us with your goodness,
and given us a place among your people.
Yet we have misused your grace,
sinned against your love
and wandered into a far country.
Therefore, Lord, from the sins that accuse us
Enfold us within the arms of your mercy,
and restore us to the company of your people,
through him in whom you have redeemed the world,
your Son our Saviour Jesus Christ. Amen.[21]

12. *The Bishop says*[22]

    May almighty God have mercy upon you,
    set you free from every bond of sin,
    and keep you in everlasting life,
    through Jesus Christ our Lord. **Amen.**[23]

13. *The Bishop goes to the penitents; greets them warmly and may embrace them.*[24]
    He leads them through the assembly while a joyful song is sung. A version of
    Psalm 34 may be suitable.

14. *The Bishop lays hands on each penitent as he/she kneels before him and says to each*
    May God the Father embrace you in his love;
    reclothe you with the purity of Christ;
    and fill you with the joy and freedom of his Spirit;
    may God give you dignity and freedom and welcome you to his table.

    Each penitent responds individually
    Amen.

---

21 After Thomas Talley in ECUSA BCP p 450
22 'In the case of the diocesan rite there are various prayers which contribute to the process of
    absolution and have their origin in various Eastern and Western prayers. In my mind this forms a
    commentary on what constitutes absolution.'
23 After Gelasian Sacramentary.
24 Originally 'embraces them, takes them by the hand and leads them . . . '. The House of Bishops
    Theological Group resisted the requirement for newly restored penitents to be embraced by the
    bishop. The Commission agreed to make it optional rather than mandatory.

The Bishop says to all the penitents

May God who pardoned David through Nathan the prophet,
may God who pardoned Peter weeping bitterly for his denial,
may God who pardoned the sinful woman shedding tears of love,
forgive you all your sins,
establish you in all goodness,
and bring you without blame or reproach before his judgement seat.
Rise, and know for certain that your sins have been forgiven.[25]

THE PEACE

15. Through the eternal Spirit Christ offered himself without blemish to God. His blood will cleanse our conscience from the deadness of our former ways to serve the living God.

The peace of the Lord be always with you.
And also with you.

The Peace is exchanged

16. *General prayers of intercession may be offered.*

17. *Where the service continues after Section 17 with the Eucharist, the following preface may be used with an authorized Eucharistic prayer.*

Worthy are you of praise and worship, God of the ages,
through Jesus Christ our Lord,
who clothed himself with the weakness of our nature
and gave his life as a ransom for our sin.
It was your will that he should destroy our death,
that he should bear our wounds in his body
and wash away our sins with his blood,
that, as we are brought low by the malice of our enemy,
so we may rise again through the victory of your Son.
Loving Lord, you accepted the tears of sinners
and promised paradise to the penitent thief,
you have welcomed home these your servants,
and restored them to the company of your saints;[26]
Therefore with angels and archangels, and with all the company of heaven,
we proclaim your great and glorious name,
for ever praising you and saying:

---

25 After the Orthodox *Order of Confession.* The word 'Rise' was inserted in the last line to give a cue to the penitents to stand for the Peace.
26 After Gelasian Sacramentary. In the April draft the fuller version of this prayer at section 18 was placed first, followed by the text for use with the eucharist. For the diocesan service, unlike the parish service, the eucharist was not mandatory.

18. *Where there is no communion all join in this thanksgiving*
Let us give thanks to the Lord our God
who is worthy of all thanksgiving and praise.

Worthy are you of praise and worship, God of the ages, through Jesus Christ our Lord, who clothed himself with the weakness of our nature and gave us his life as a ransom for our sin. It was your will that he should destroy our death, that he should bear our wounds in his body and wash away our sins with his blood, that, as we are brought low by the malice of our enemy, so we may rise again through the victory of your Son. Loving Lord, as you accepted the tears of sinners and promised paradise to the penitent thief, so welcome home these your servants, restore them to the company of your saints, and let not the enemy triumph over them. May your Son reconcile them to yourself and welcome them once more to his banquet. May he renew them with his body and blood and lead them to the joy of heaven, where he is alive and reigns with you and the Holy Spirit, one God, world without end. **Blessed be God for ever. Amen**

CONCLUSION

19. *A hymn of praise and thanksgiving is sung*

20. *The Bishop gives the blessing and dismisses the assembly*

(c) A PARISH RITE
(AN ORDER FOR RECONCILIATION AND RESTORATION AT A CELEBRATION OF HOLY COMMUNION)

INTRODUCTORY NOTES
1. This order may be appropriately used where serious and public sin, either individual or corporate, has done grievous damage to the health and *witness* of a congregation or where members of the congregation have been in open hostility with each other.
2. Where it is proposed that a person or persons be kept from the Lord's Table the bishop is to be informed and his direction followed (see Canon B16).
3. In the case of individual sin the person or people concerned shall receive appropriate counselling and pastoral care. The order shall not be used until every effort has been made to put right what has gone wrong and there is good reason to believe that those concerned are established in a stable pattern of life. The service shall be prepared by a group that includes at least one person nominated by those who are to receive the laying on of hands with prayer. No person shall be forced to take part without their free consent.
4. Where the rite is used to address a breakdown of pastoral relationships that affects a whole Christian community, the President may appropriately be Rural Dean or Archdeacon, using the forms of Sections 11, 12 and 16 set out in the Appendix.
5. The content of any confession made shall under no circumstances be disclosed to anyone without the consent of the person concerned. Where appropriate, a form of words may be agreed and used in the rite. Such a statement should not go beyond a brief and general statement of the matter concerned.

PREPARATION

1. *At the entrance of the ministers a psalm, hymn or chant may be sung*

2. *THE GREETING*

   Grace, mercy and peace from God our Father and the Lord Jesus Christ be
   with you
   And also with you.

3. *PENITENCE*

   In silence let us all call to mind our sins and the overflowing grace of God.

   Silence is kept

   God shows his love for us
   in that while we were yet sinners Christ died for us.
   Lord have mercy.
   Lord have mercy.

   By one Spirit we have all been baptized into one body.
   If one member suffers, all suffer together.
   Christ have mercy.
   Christ have mercy.

   Through the obedience of the one man Jesus Christ
   the many are made righteous in the kingdom of life.
   Lord have mercy.
   Lord have mercy.

4. *THE COLLECT*

THE MINISTRY OF THE WORD

5. *OLD TESTAMENT READING*[27]

6. *A psalm or canticle may be sung*

7. *NEW TESTAMENT READING*

8. *A hymn or canticle may be sung*

9. *THE GOSPEL*

10. *THE SERMON*[28]

---

27 Again, in the April draft, readings now in the table at the end were set out here, but it was also
made clear that the readings of the day could be used.
28 The April text allows for the Nicene Creed at this point.

19

THE CELEBRATION OF FORGIVENESS

11. *The people sit and the priest says*
Brothers and sisters in Christ, none of us is righteous of ourselves and all of us need the forgiveness which Christ has made available to us through his death and resurrection. Jesus did not come to condemn the world but that the world might be saved though him. In the face of sin we are not to despair but to embrace the love and forgiveness which God has pledged to us in our baptism. Today our *brother/sister* seeks our prayer and support as *he/she* turns away from sin and seeks God's grace to make a new start in the Christian way.

    In preparing for this day *he/she has* opened *his/her life* to the support and counsel of others and *has* sought the grace of God in fasting and prayer. It is now our privilege to extend to *him/her* the welcoming and forgiving grace of God, and so to rejoice together in the forgiveness which is ours in Jesus Christ.

12. *The person or people concerned stand before the assembly and say*
People of God, *I/we* acknowledge before God and before you,
my/our brothers and sisters in Christ,
that *I/we* have fallen into sin *[where agreed, a particular matter may be mentioned]*. Trusting in the love and mercy of God,
I/we now seek your prayers
that *I/we* may be strengthened
to serve God in holiness from this day forward.[29]

13. *The priest says*

    Since we all sin and fail short of the glory of God,
    let us kneel in silence and pray for the grace and forgiveness of God.

    Silence is kept

14. **Father eternal, giver of light and grace,**
we have sinned against you and against our neighbour,
in what we have thought,
in what we have said and done,
through ignorance, through weakness,
through our own deliberate fault.
We have wounded your love,
and marred your image in us.
We are sorry and ashamed,
and repent of all our sins.
For the sake of your Son Jesus Christ, who died for us,
forgive us all that is past;
and lead us out from darkness
to walk as children of light. Amen.

---

29 After Oliver O'Donovan in *Ethics and Liturgy* (see pp 6-7 above).

15. *The priest says the absolution using this form or any other authorized form of absolution:*

God who is both power and love,
forgive you and free you from your sins,
heal and strengthen you by his Spirit,
and raise you to new life in Christ our Lord. **Amen.**[30]

16. *All stand and the penitent(s) kneel before the priest. The priest and one or two others lay hands on each person. The priest says one of these two prayers*

Either

May God in his love create in you a clean heart, and renew a right spirit
   within you.
May his Holy Spirit live within you and give you the joy of his salvation,
through Jesus Christ our Lord. **Amen.**

or

May God the Father embrace you in his love;
reclothe you with the purity of Christ,
and fill you with the joy of his Spirit;
may God give you dignity and freedom
and welcome you to his table. **Amen.**

17. *The Penitents also stand and all say the following thanksgiving:*

Behold, now is the acceptable time.
Now is the day of salvation.

God was in Christ reconciling the world to himself
not counting our sins against us.

As the heavens are high above the earth
so great is his love towards those who fear him.

As far as the east is from the west
so far does he remove our sins from us.

All this is from God, who reconciles us to himself through Christ
and has given us the ministry of reconciliation

Christ died for all so that we who live may live not for ourselves
but for Christ who died and rose again for us.[31]

---

30 Authorized in *A Service of the Word*, Absolution 4.
31 2 Corinthians 5, Psalm 103.

THE PEACE

18. We are the body of Christ
In the one Spirit we were all baptized into one body.
Let us then pursue all that makes for peace
and builds up our common life.

The peace of the Lord be always with you.
And also with you.

The Peace is exchanged.

19. *A hymn may be sung.*

20. *The Eucharist continues with the intercession, and the Preparation of the Gifts. It may be appropriate for the holy table to be prepared in silence with quiet music.*

21. *The following preface may be used with an authorized Eucharistic prayer.*

Worthy are you of praise and worship
through Jesus Christ our Lord,
who clothed himself with the weakness of our nature
and gave his life as a ransom for our sin.
It was your will that he should destroy our death,
that he should bear our wounds in his body
and wash away our sins with his blood,
that, as we are brought low by the malice of the enemy,
so we may rise again through the victory of your Son.
Loving Lord, you accepted the tears of sinners
and promised paradise to the penitent thief,
you welcome home those who fall into sin,
and restore them to the company of your saints;
Therefore with angels and archangels, and with all the company of heaven,
we proclaim your great and glorious name,
for ever praising you and saying:[32]

APPENDIX: FORMS OF SECTIONS 11, 12 AND 16 TO BE USED WITH A WHOLE CHRISTIAN COMMUNITY

11. *The priest says*

Brothers and sisters in Christ, none of us is righteous of ourselves and all of us need the forgiveness which Christ has made available to us through his death and resurrection. Jesus did not come to condemn the world but that the world might be saved through him.

---

[32] Gelasian Sacramentary, adapted, as p 17 above.

Jesus did not come to condemn the world but that the world might be saved through him. In the face of sin we are not to despair but to embrace the love and forgiveness which God has pledged to us in our baptism. Today we pray for one another as we turn from our past sin and seek God's grace to make a new start in the Christian way.

In preparing for this day we have tried to share together our understanding of our past failings and sought the grace of God in prayer and thoughtfulness. It is now our privilege to share in the forgiving grace of God, made known to us in Jesus Christ, our Lord.

12. *All say*

**We acknowledge before God
that in ignorance, by carelessness
and through deliberate word and deed
we have fallen into sin.
Trusting in the love and mercy of God
we now pray for one another
that together we may be strengthened
to serve God in holiness from this day forward.**

16 *Each person in turn kneels before the priest, who lays hands on each and says*
[continue as in main text]

(d) FORMS FOR INDIVIDUAL RECONCILIATION

INTRODUCTORY NOTES
1. These orders may be appropriately used when a person's conscience is burdened with a particular sin, when a person wishes to make a new beginning in the Christian life, or as part of a regular personal discipline.
2. The Book of Common Prayer includes the following pastoral exhortation:
    — if there be any of you, who by this means [self-examination, confession and repentance] cannot quiet his own conscience herein, but requireth further comfort or counsel, let him come to me, or to some other discreet and learned Minister of God's Word, and open his grief; that by the ministry of God's holy Word he may receive the benefit of absolution, together with ghostly counsel and advice, to the quieting of his conscience, and avoiding of all scruple and doubtfulness.
    The aim of such a ministry of comfort and counsel is to establish an individual in the freedom and forgiveness of Christ. It can be exercised in a variety of ways at the discretion of the minister, the authorisation of these two orders is not intended to limit such discretion.
3. The reconciliation of a penitent, even when celebrated privately remains a corporate action of the church because sin affects the unity of the body; through the absolution the penitent is restored to full fellowship in Christ. Two forms of this rite are provided. The first form is more simple and follows a familiar pattern in the Western church. The second form draws on other traditions of reconciliation.
4. In giving advice to the penitent the priest should encourage restitution where this is appropriate and may recommend some prayer or action as a token of repentance.
5. Each form consists of three parts: Introduction, Confession and Counsel, and Reconciliation. The first and second parts of these forms may be used as part of an individual's preparation for any public celebration of reconciliation.
6. The minister who is entrusted with a confession is forbidden by Canon Law from making known its content to any person whatsoever. The content of a confession is not a matter of subsequent discussion except on the initiative of the penitent. The name of a partner in sin must not be mentioned or enquired after.

23

FIRST FORM

INTRODUCTION

The priest welcomes the penitent and together they prepare for the celebration of this ministry. The priest may say:
In the name of the Father, and of the Son, and of the Holy Spirit. **Amen.**

This is a saying you can trust:
God in his mercy has saved us
through the washing and rebirth and renewal by the Holy Spirit,
so that with hope we may enter the life of the kingdom.
May the Lord be in your heart and on your lips
that you may know the truth that sets us free
and confess your sins with true sorrow. **Amen.**

A passage of scripture is read

CONFESSION AND COUNSEL

Christ is present with us:
he looks on your sorrow and hears your prayer,
Therefore open your heart
and confess your sins to him with confidence in his mercy.

I confess to almighty God,
before the whole company of heaven,
and you my *brother/sister*
that I have sinned in thought, word and deed,
and in what I have left undone . . .

Here the penitent confesses particular sins
For these and all other sins which I cannot now remember,
I pray for God's grace and ask forgiveness.

The priest may, with the consent of the penitent, offer words of comfort and counsel.

RECONCILIATION

The priest invites the penitent to express sorrow and repentance in his or her own words or by using one of the following:

A
Have mercy on me, O God, according to your loving kindness;
In your great compassion blot out my offences.
Wash me through and through from my wickedness
and cleanse me from my sin.
Create in me a clean heart, O God,
and renew a right spirit within me.

24

B
I am sorry and ashamed,
and repent of all my sins.
For the sake of your Son Jesus Christ,
who died for me,
forgive me all that is past;
and lead me out from darkness
to walk in the light of life. Amen.

The priest lays hands on, or extends hands over, the penitent and says the absolution.
The priest may use one of the following or any other authorized form of absolution:

God who is both power and love,
forgive you and free you from your sins,
heal and strengthen you by his Spirit,
and raise you to new life in Christ our Lord. **Amen.**

or

Our Lord Jesus Christ
who, in the power of the resurrection,
entrusts the Spirit of reconciliation to his church,
forgives you and frees you from the bonds of sin:
as a sign and witness of his redeeming love,
I absolve you from all your sins,
in the name of the Father, and of the Son, and of the Holy Spirit. **Amen.**[33]

Either or both the following may be said:

Merciful God,
We thank you that you have delivered
this your servant from the power of sin
and restored *him/her* to your peace
in the fellowship of the Church;
strengthen *him/her* by your Spirit
that *he/she* may please you
until *he/she* comes to the fullness of your eternal kingdom;
through Jesus Christ our Lord. **Amen.**

[Or]

Praise the Lord O my soul
all my being, bless his holy name.
He forgives all our sins
and heals all our diseases.
He redeems our life from the grave
and crowns us with mercy and love.

---

[33]   This is the text outlined in Gordon Jeanes' article below.

The priest dismisses the penitent using one of the following:

> The Lord has put away your sins.
> **Thanks be to God.**
>
> Go in peace and pray for me a sinner.

or

> The Lord has freed you from your sins.
> Go now in peace and joy,
> to proclaim in the world
> the wonderful works of God.
> Amen. Thanks be to God.

The priest may add

> Pray also for me a sinner.

SECOND FORM

INTRODUCTION

The priest welcomes the penitent and together they prepare for the celebration of this ministry

The priest may say:

> Blessed be the God and Father of our Lord Jesus Christ.
> By his great mercy we have been born anew to a living hope
> through the resurrection of Jesus Christ from the dead.
> **Blessed be God for ever.**

A brief silence is kept. Then priest and penitent say together one of the following

A   The Lord is good to all;
     His compassion rests on all that he has made.
     The Lord is near to all who call to him;
     To all who call to him in sincerity.
     The Lord fulfils the desire of all who fear him;
     He hears their cry and saves them.[34]

---

21 Psalm 145.

B   The Lord is full of compassion and mercy,
slow to anger and of great kindness.
He will not always accuse us,
nor will he keep his anger for ever.
He has not dealt with us according to our sins,
nor rewarded us according to our wickedness.
As a father cares for his children,
so does the Lord care for those who fear him,
For he himself knows of what we are made;
he remembers that we are but dust.[35]

C   Have mercy on me, O God, according to your loving-kindness;
in your great compassion blot out my offences.
Wash me through and through from my wickedness
and cleanse me from my sin.
Create in me a clean heart, O God,
and renew a right spirit within me.
Cast me not away from your presence
and take not your holy Spirit from me.
Give me the joy of your saving help again
and sustain me with your bountiful Spirit.
Open my lips, O Lord,
and my mouth shall proclaim your praise.[36]

CONFESSION AND COUNSEL

Have faith in God who is steadfast in love and infinite in mercy,
healing the sick and forgiving the sinful.
May God, who enlightens every heart,
help you to confess your sins and to trust in his mercy.[37]

Holy and loving God,
from dust you have formed me in your likeness,
and redeemed me from death by your cross;
by water and Spirit
you have washed away my sins,
clothed me with your goodness,
and given me a place among your people .
Yet I have misused your grace, sinned against your love
and wandered into a far country.

---

35 Psalm 103.
36 Psalm 51
37 Adapted from [Canadian] *Book of Alternative Services* [BAS] which adapted it from the Roman
Catholic service.

Especially I confess.

Here the penitent confesses particular sins.

**Therefore, Lord, from the sins that accuse *me*,
I turn to you in sorrow and repentance.
Enfold me within the arms of your mercy,
and restore me to the company of your people,
through him in whom you have redeemed the world,
your Son our Saviour Jesus Christ. Amen.**[38]

The priest may, with the consent of the penitent, offer words of comfort and counsel

The priest may read an appropriate passage of scripture[39]

RECONCILIATION
Do you turn again to Christ?
I turn to Christ.
Do you forgive those who have sinned against you?
I forgive them.[40]

*The priest lays hands on, or extends hands over, the penitent and says the absolution.
The priest may use one of the following or any other authorized form of absolution*

The Lord Jesus Christ,
Lamb of God and our great high priest,
who shares our human nature
and stands for us at God's right hand,
set you free from all your sins by his Holy Spirit
and establish you again among his people. **Amen.**[41]

38 After Thomas Talley in ECUSA BCP p 450. The 2004 service returns almost completely to Talley's
    original (Talley differences italicized):
      Holy God, heavenly Father,
      you formed me from the dust in your image and likeness,
      and redeemed me from sin and death
      by the cross of your Son Jesus Christ.
      Through the water of baptism you clothed me
      with the shining garment of *his* righteousness,
      and established me among your children in your kingdom.
      But I have squandered the inheritance of your saints
      and have wandered (*far in a land that is waste*) in a far country.
      Especially, I confess to you and before the Church ...

      Therefore, O Lord, from these and all other sins I cannot *now* remember,
      I turn in sorrow and repentance.
      Receive me again into the arms of your mercy,
      and restore me to the blessed company of your faithful people;
      through him in whom you have redeemed the world,
      your Son our Saviour, Jesus Christ.
39 MV's note simply says '(1552/1662!)'
40 BAS p 168
41 inspired—very roughly!—by the Orthodox rite and BCP-USA p 451.

or

God the Father of mercies,
through his Son Jesus Christ
forgives all who truly repent and believe in him:
by the ministry of reconciliation
which Christ has committed to his Church,
and in the power of his Spirit,
I declare that you are absolved from your sins,
in the name of the Father,
and of the Son, and of the Holy Spirit. **Amen.**[42]

CONCLUSION

Priest and penitent join in thanksgiving

Know that there is joy in heaven over each one who repents

As the heavens are high above the earth.
so great is God's love towards those who fear him.

As far as the east is from the west,
so far does he remove our sins from us.

The Lord has put away your sin,
Thanks be to God.

Go in peace and pray for me a sinner.

TABLE OF READINGS

1. Forgiveness and Reconciliation

a) Old Testament	b) New Testament	c) Gospel
Jeremiah 3 1.31-34	2 Corinthians 2.5-11	Luke 15.1-10
Ezekiel 34.11-16	Colossians 1.15-23a	Luke 15.11-32
Ezekiel 37.1-14	New Testament	Luke 23.32-43
Colossians 2.9-15	John 11.1-44	
	1 Peter 2.19-25	

2. Reconciliation within context of Holy Communion

a) Old Testament	b) New Testament Reading	c) Gospel
Deut 15.7-15	Psalm 32. 103.1-14	Matthew 18.12-14[-20]
Deut 30.1-10 [-14]	Romans 14.4-12	Matthew 18.21-35
2 Sam 12.7-13	2 Corinthians 2.5-11	Mark 2.1-12
1 Kings 8.33-40	2 Corinthians 5.14-6.2	
	2 Corinthians 7.8-13	Luke 7.36-50
		Luke 15.1-10
Isaiah 42.1-9	Galatians 6.1-5	Luke 23.32-43
Isaiah 49.14-23	1 John 1.5-9	
Isaiah 44.21-23	James 5.13-18 [-20]	John 1.24-34
Isaiah 54.4-10		John 3.3-14
	Revelation 3.14-22	John 13.31-35
Jeremiah 31.31-34	Revelation 12.7-12	
Hosea 14.1-7		John 20. 19-23
Zech 3		John 21.15-17 [-23]

---

[42] Originally commended in *Lent, Holy Week, Easter* (1986), p 56, this was authorized in *A Service of the Word*, Absolution 11.

4
Guilt And Pastoral Care
by Gordon Oliver

Obvious Connection?

At first sight the connection between guilt and the Rite of Reconciliation is the most obvious in the world. People who are troubled in conscience because they know or feel themselves to be guilty before God 'come to confession' to seek forgiveness. What could in principle be simpler? Such a view has the advantage of more than a thousand years of the Church's official and lived theology and of popular perception behind it. The sacrament of penance was officially described, locally applied and personally appropriated in terms which had all of the hallmarks of law, judgement and satisfaction about them. Certainly the personal pastoral dimension has been present too. Priests who have heard confessions have frequently done so with great sensitivity. Penitents have often derived real release and comfort from having been received with respect and heard with a carefulness that gave space for sorrow without self-pity or sentimentality. They have been sent on their way strengthened in their sense of unity with God and his Church by the authoritative word of absolution.

The sacrament of penance, throughout its history, has had to wrestle with this tension between a theology of pastoral care seen as the application of moral law and the practice of pastoral care seen as the nurture of persons.[43] One may propose that it has moved furthest from the central heart of the Gospel when it has failed to recognize that such a tension is there at all. Where the application of the sacrament has been routinised, or where its moral theological base has ceased to attract the allegiance of large numbers of the community of the faithful, the rite is increasingly found to embody not return and acceptance, but distance and alienation. The confusion in the Roman Catholic Church about the right relationship of this sacrament to the moral framework of ordinary life, and the virtual official absence of the sacrament from the provision of the Church of England, has tended to foster this distancing. There can be few experiences more personally boring or spiritually debilitating than bearing one's guilt or one's shame alone, but that is in fact the experience of large numbers of christians in both Roman Catholic and Protestant Churches at the end of the 20th century.

In this chapter we will explore the connection between guilt and pastoral care by attending first to some of the main confusions surrounding the experience of guilt, and of the social and theological context of guilt. We will briefly consider the importance of the role that may be played by ritual in pastoral care. Following this we will explore the shape and agenda of pastoral care and its role in relation to people experiencing guilt. Finally we will comment on the creative pastoral

---

43 An excellent and accessible exposition of the history and recent development of the Rite of Penance and Sacrament of Reconciliation is James Dallen, *The Reconciling Community : The Rite of Penance* (The Liturgical Press, Collegeville, Minnesota, 1986).

opportunities offered by reconciliation rites for the renewal of people and of communities.

What Kind of People are Guilty People?

Guilt is a rather slippery term to try to get hold of because the word is used to describe both a state of affairs and an emotion or feeling that may or may not have anything to do with things as they actually are. For instance Burglar Bill may be caught red handed and found guilty in a court. He is guilty whether or not he feels any sense of guilt. Burglar Bill's wife, Betty may feel deeply ashamed and guilty about the crime committed by her husband. She did not commit the crime. She is not actually guilty before the law, but she carries within herself a sense of being guilty for his wrongdoing. Their neighbours, who have been victims of Bill's nocturnal visits, reinforce Betty's guilt-feelings by the comments they make and the way they treat her and her children when they go out. But the same neighbours are also on the receiving end of guilt projections as people across the other side of town read about Bill's crime in the papers, and ask one another what else you can expect of folk living in such a rough area where 'those kind of people' are always in trouble. In fact it's fairly common for the people in Bill's community to feel guilty without any particular reason just because of where they live.

From this example we can see some of the different ways the world *guilt* is commonly used. When it describes Bill's conviction its meaning is plain, but in relation to the other people we may be dealing with a whole variety of experience that would better be described as neurosis, victimisation, accusation, and social disintegration. The pastoral tasks in relation to each of these different groups may be very different and include legal processes, befriending, counselling, psychotherapy, spiritual direction, sacramental reconciliation, community work and political action. A pastoral care strategy which attends to only one such area, without awareness of the possible importance of the others, is likely to be satisfying in the short term and spiritually barren in the longer perspective.[44]

All of this is complex enough, but we may think that as long as we all consider that burglary is wrong, we may satisfy ourselves that we can find a way through. But the problem is compounded because the social context within which we use the language of guilt is also multi-faceted. Recent decades have seen large shifts in attitudes in the affluent west towards issues of personal and communal morality and in the perception of what is or is not acceptable behaviour. The public battles between groups claiming to speak for the 'moral majority' and those seeking broader interpretations of public freedom, show that the traffic is not universally moving in one direction. The subject matter of conflicting opinions is wide ranging indeed, with the financial, communal, sexual and gender agendas

---

44 Two useful treatments of these issues are: May Anne Coat, *Sin, Guilt and Forgiveness*, (SPCK, London, 1994), which uses a series of case stories to explore the variety of pastoral, spiritual and moral issues that need to be taken into account in dealing with people wrestling with guilt; and Dorin Barter, *Grace Abounding : Wrestling with Sin and Guilt* (DLT, London, 1993), which explores the relationship between spirituality and psychology in relation to guilt.

high on the list. Perhaps the Church can act as friend and guide in this confused and confusing scene.

However, Christians seeking reassurance or guidance have a love-hate relationship with the way the Church does or does not make clear statements about what is or is not acceptable as an expression of christian discipleship. Thus the papal encyclical *Humanae Vitae* (1968) gave clear guidance to Roman Catholics about (*inter alia*) artificial birth control, whilst attracting a heaping of scorn on the Church's teaching authority from many sources for more than two decades. The Church of England tends to fare little better, not least because her approach tends more toward an open-ended exposition of issues of public and personal morality, which is intended to put the responsibility for decisions about right belief and right conduct within the individual believer's sphere of freedom to decide. One effect of this, at least publicly, is to make the Church of England appear indecisive and unclear about moral values.

The increasing emphasis since the Second World War on the rights and responsibilities of the individual have had the effect of replacing external and 'given' authority structures that could offer support and guidance, with two other, and frequently competing, emphases. The external authority of the church's teaching and guidance has been replaced by the internalised authority (which was of course never absent) of individual conscience; and the community of believers supporting and encouraging one another has been replaced with a 'wider reference community and the attachment of guilt to values more pluralistically and idiosyncratically construed.[45] At the same time as offering the individual the illusion of being part of a great community of responsible adults, the effect of these shifts has been to foster an increasing sense of isolation and alienation. Lehman describes 'the "decline" and "fall" of conscience . . . this mushrooming individualization of conscience has led to a growing sense of moral isolation of guilt-in-a-vacuum, of narcissistic or solipsistic decision making.'[46]

Theological Agenda

Throughout the Bible guilt is taken with utmost seriousness as a clear sign of alienation from God, the community of God's people, and from oneself. Guilt is the natural consequence of the presence of sin. In this sense guilt in the Bible is like pain in the body — good and useful because it points to something that is wrong and that needs urgently to be put right. Key to understanding the interpretation of guilt in the Bible is the notion of sin as violation of the covenant. The freedom of the covenant community and its members is to be found in the fulfilment of their calling to live in obedience and dependence upon the God who saves. In Deuteronomy 11.18-32 the blessing and prosperity of God's people is conditional upon them entering the freedom of the land of God's promise, by the route God has opened up (crossing the Jordan) such that 'when you occupy

---

45 Article 'Guilt' by E.V. Stein in Rodney J. Hunter (ed), *Dictionary of Pastoral Care and Counselling* (Abingdon, Nashville, 1990) p 487.
46 *ibid.*

it and live in it, you must diligently observe all the statutes and ordinances that I am setting before you today.' (verses 31-32).[47]

When the covenant is violated the welfare of the community as well as of the individual is put at risk (Joshua 7), and the way provided in the deuteronomic code for dealing with sin is through the ritual of sacrificial renewal, especially that linked with the day of atonement. This reflects guilt as a state of affairs irrespective of the emotions of the individual and the remedy for guilt is the determined, devoted obedient action of sacrifice. By majoring on the interpretation of the cross of Jesus Christ as atoning sacrifice, the New Testament writers place the remedy for the guilt separation brought about by sin, firmly within the objective realm. (see e.g. 1 Corinthians 5.7-8 ; 1 Peter 2.23-25). The cross is, in a primary sense, 'out there' in relation to the life of the Christian disciple. (John 12.31-32)—a point which is emphasized by the way the Gospel writers surround the crucifixion scene with a whole array of witnesses and commentators, including Mary herself, the beloved disciple, soldiers, servants, onlookers, thieves, fellow victims.

But if there is an 'out-thereness' of the cross which reflects the objectivity of guilt and human need before God, there is also an 'in-hereness' about guilt in the Bible. The classic Old Testament reference to this is Psalm 51.3-5:

> For I know my transgressions,
> and my sin is ever before me.
> Against you, you alone, have I sinned
> and done what is evil in your sight,
> so that you are justified in your sentence
> and blameless when you pass judgement.
> Indeed, I was born guilty,
> a sinner when my mother conceived me.

This passage encapsulates the experience of guilt before God as the clear state of affairs, as raw emotion, and as a sense of being alienated and in need of God's mercy in one's very being, irrespective of any action having been committed. Here we have the experience of guilt, shame and dread—an unholy trinity— woven together into a rope that holds the sinner in its coils.[48]

The New Testament also reflects the 'in-hereness' of this experience of being tied up by guilt and shame. St. Paul wrestles with the agony of knowing that 'I do not do the good I want, but the evil that I do not want is what I do . . . Wretched man that I am! Who will deliver me from this body of death?' (Romans 7.19, 24). The liberation of the cross for Paul is precisely bound up with the fact that its 'out-thereness' and its 'in-hereness' serve directly and clearly to address the condition of being tied up in the guilt of covenant violation. He cries out with joy, 'Thanks be to God through Jesus Christ our Lord' (Romans 7.25a) because he has been caught

---

47   Bible quotations are from The New Revised Standard Version.
48   In the social anthropology literature there was a tendency to divide primitive (*sic*) societies into those expressing guilt cultures and those expressing shame cultures. This division is now widely questioned though the differentiation between the experience and states of being guilty and bearing shame is an important and useful one.

up in experience by the vision of what the cross of Jesus means as atonement and as liberation.'I have been crucified with Christ; and it is no longer I who live, but it is Christ who lives in me. And the life I now live, I live by faith in the Son of God who loved me and gave himself for me.' (Galatians 2.19-20).

It is important to recognise that the NT Epistles, giving full weight as they do to the saving power of the death of Jesus Christ, spend by far the majority of their space addressing issues of membership and behaviour of the Christian communities to whom they are addressed (something like 90% in the case of the Corinthian letters). This reflects as clearly as could be the continuation from its Jewish roots of the theology of guilt as violation of the covenant and of the covenant community. It reflects, therefore, the agenda for reconciliation as reconciliation of the sinner with God in Christ and therefore with the church as the community of the new covenant—the community of reconciliation (2 Corinthians 5.18-21). At the heart of this is the unshakeable reality that the Christian is one who in transforming repentance (*metanoia*) has been baptized into the living and dying and rising of Jesus Christ (Romans 6.1-11). The ministry of reconciliation is about living out, and living out of this conversion. Reconciliation is fundamentally about the reaffirmation of a person's belonging with God in Christ in the covenant community—the people redeemed and liberated to proclaim in deed and word Christ's saving grace for the life of the world. Thus reconciliation in the covenant community is decisively linked with the vocation to share in God's mission in the world (1 Peter 2.9-10).

This objective and interior, and communal and personal, theology of God's saving grace for the world is what lies at the root of the development of the ministry of reconciliation of penitents through the early Chrisitan centuries and into present times. The ministry of pastoral care with guilty people finds its roots in this biblical and historical tradition, and lives out its calling in the confused and confusing context outlined above.

The Importance of Ritual

From the beginning the Christian Church has found itself uneasy about some aspects of spiritual ritual at the same time as being committed to the proper celebration of ritual. The unease arose initially from the increasing distancing of the growing Church from its roots in Judaism. The difficulties the different communities of believers had in seeking agreement about which rituals were to be retained are documented in Acts 15.1-21, and the heat they generated then and subsequently is radiated in Galatians 2.11-14. The early Christians were, however, not without ritual, as the central importance of the two dominical sacraments, baptism and eucharist, testifies. The growth of pastoral ritual in relation to the initiation and reconciliation of penitents is well documented.

People in the Church of England bring a rather well honed hermeneutic of suspicion to the issue of ritual in public worship and pastoral ministry. The Reformation split with Rome and internal disputes since, especially the 19th century ritual controversies, have served to stoke the fires of unease. Nevertheless we need to get clear that as human beings, particularly perhaps as human beings seeking to worship and serve God in the world, we have no choice about *whether* we engage in ritual, only about *what* ritual we engage in and how.

Writers about ritual from Arnold van Gennep[49] to Maurice Bloch[50] are agreed that the purpose of ritual is the transformation of persons. Rituals are not about magic, they are the expressions of the beliefs, values, hopes and purposes of communities. They are means of giving shape to, of embodying, the word of transformation. There are many features of the contribution of rituals to the lives of people and communities.[51] Among the most important for our purposes are that good pastoral rituals enable the setting of boundaries of behaviour and belonging; establish or re-establish the identity of persons; bring a sense of order that can contain the volatile emotions of personal and community chaos; enable communities to identify their purpose and renew their vision. Rituals enable the transformation of persons by giving someone who is (say) guilty, or bereaved a sort of acted journey or pilgrimage from the place where they became separated from their personal relationships or spiritual roots; through a period of transition where what is being left is clarified and bidden farewell to and what is being moved toward is recognised and welcomed; and permission to move into a new or renewed state of being and belonging. In a word, ritual is all about embodiment of hope, purpose and transformation.

It is extraordinary that many Christians who would never dream of baptizing their children, marrying their young or burying their dead without proper recognition that is embodied in worship and ritual, would be ready to deny to their fellow believers the opportunity for reconciliation through the use of worship and ritual within the Christian community. There is a real need in the Church of England for us to move decisively away from this sense of unease, in order to release the opportunity for ritual to make its proper contribution.

One of the important features of community rituals is that although their finer points may not all be written down, their main structures and purposes are in a very real sense *prescribed*. That is to say that the ritual is not just dreamed up on a whim, but that engagement in the ritual involves recognition that we belong to a people who really are the people of God—who share the life of the world-wide Christian community. It can be seen why it is important for the pastoral care of Christians and for the integrity and mission of the Church, that there are available Rites of Reconciliation which embody the values, care and purposes which we share.[52] There are encouraging indications of a much greater awareness of the importance of pastoral ritual across the range of church traditions[53], which

---

49 Arnold Van Gennep, *Rites of Passage* (Paris, 1906).

50 Maurice Bloch, *Prey into Hunter : The Politics of Religious Experience* (Cambridge University Press, 1992).

51 See e.g. Tom F. Driver, *The Magic of Ritual : Our Need for Liberating Rites that Transform our Lives and our Communities* (Harper Collins, San Francisco, 1991) (see esp. pp 195-222).

52 A useful study of the pastoral use of ritual is Elaine Ramshaw, *Ritual and Pastoral Care* (Fortress Press, Philadelphia, 1987).

53 See e.g. Hannah Ward and Jennifer Wild (compilers), *Human Rites : Worship Resources for an Age of Change* (Mowbray, London, 1995).

may indicate that the time is now ripe for the Church of England to take the Rites of Reconciliation into its liturgical and pastoral life.

The Shape of Pastoral Care

While in the Roman Catholic Church the shape of, and the agenda for, pastoral care has, until recent times been (at least theoretically) clear, finding its primary focus in the ministry of the Sacraments validly celebrated and the ministry of the Word authoritatively taught and preached, the same cannot be said about the Church of England. Here, notwithstanding the historic formularies, clarity about the aims and methods of pastoral care has been very dependent on which strands of the *catholic and reformed* traditions within our Church govern the local expression of its life. The puritan emphasis on pastoral care as the ministry and discipline of the Word brought home, the catholic emphasis on personal commitment to sacramental care and community service, the charismatic emphasis on fellowship and emotional integrity, the liberal emphasis on releasing the believer for living the gospel in the world, and mixtures of all of these and others besides, find their expression among us.[54] In this sense the shape of, and agenda for, pastoral care in the Church of England has been very much what the local church decides that it will be.

Within this eclecticism, there have been a number of major trends since the late 1960s, though their roots are to be found much further back. Prominent among them has been pastoral care as social action and, more dominantly recently, pastoral care as the quest for personal healing. Both of these trends, whilst attending to groups of key issues which Christians must face, have tended to leave the theological roots of christian pastoral ministry unexplored and progressively assumed, rather than expressed. The 'gut feeling' has been that as Christians we must be committed to justice for the world, and that we must urgently seek the healing and welfare of suffering people. This is the theological equivalent of 'mum and home and apple pie'. We are all in favour, but if we do not establish our key theological purposes we are likely to lose both a sense of vision for developing our pastoral ministry and a means of subjecting our action to proper scrutiny.

I want to propose three foundational truths about Christian pastoral care which will serve to promote the self-consciousness of people engaged in this ministry.

1. Pastoral Care finds its True Vocation in serving the Purposes of God as they are revealed in Jesus Christ.
This may seem almost ridiculously obvious. But the wide ranging nature of Christian pastoral care and the diffuseness of its means and methods frequently leads to the assumption of generalized and ultimately purposeless 'do gooding',

---

54 Of course these emphases are also present in the Roman Catholic Church, but my point relates to how authority is interpreted in relation to the pastoral care agenda.

which can easily sap the energy and morale of the practitioners. This is a particularly acute problem in the protestant traditions.

The NT Gospels are full of the preaching of Jesus about the coming of the Kingdom of God, the Kingdom of Heaven, the drawing near of his 'hour' and the nearness of his 'glory'. This preaching is addressed to an expressed in the language and experience of earthy suffering and of heaven-bent liberation, both at the same time. Jesus' direct association of himself with the proclamation of Isaiah 61.1ff in the synagogue at Nazareth (Luke 4.16ff); his reply to the question of the imprisoned John the Baptist (Luke 7.18-23); the parable of the last judgement (Matthew 25.31-46) and the 'I am' sayings in John's Gospel all bear testimony to an essential direction of the purpose of the revelation of God in Jesus Christ. The OT resonances and the NT contexts of all of these passages and metaphors point directly to a ministry of salvation through the route of a new Exodus. This salvation brings a re-rooted relationship of the person and the community with the living God. It depends ultimately on the transformation of mind and purpose (*metanoia*) that comes through allegiance to Jesus Christ living, dying, rising, calling. One of the reasons why the NT writers are so concerned with the issues of right behaviour and right relationships in the infant church, is because they can see so clearly the connection between salvation, truth, integrity and the effectiveness of the community of believers engaging in witness to the Gospel of Christ (cf Philippians 3.12-4.7; 1 John 1.1-10).

2. Christian Pastoral Care is Part and Parcel of Christian Mission

Although healing, counselling, social and political action, etc. may all be expressions of Christian pastoral care, none of them finds its identity as *Christian* pastoral care unless its ultimate aim is to express the mission of God as revealed in Jesus Christ.[55] That is to say that healing, social action, etc. may properly be understood as *signs* of the kingdom, but they are not *in themselves* the coming of the kingdom. Certainly the purposes of God are worked out in the lives of people and among communities, but these are themselves part of a yet bigger picture. A good example of this is the structure of the letter of the Ephesians. At the beginning the writer wrestles to put into words the purpose of God 'in the fullness of time, to gather all things in him, things in heaven and things on earth.' This is then worked out through relationships between rival parts of the Christian community, the call to servanthood with integrity, attention to issues of marriage, parenthood and employment, and the call to resist the assaults of evil in the strength of the Lord.

Certainly, mission has many different facets ranging from the direct preaching of the Gospel in evangelism to less obviously 'missionary' activities which may involve teaching, guiding, sustaining, healing, social and political action, etc. Mission, to be genuinely Christian, will need to attend to the gospel

---

55 The idea of God having attributes of movement and development and engaging in mission is a major theme of the later work of Jurgen Moltmann. A flavour of this can be gained from the section 'The End of Space in the Presence of God' in Jurgen Moltmann, *The Coming of God* (SCM, London, 1996) pp 296-308.

environment—physical, relational, sociological, political, psychological, spiritual—as well as to directly churchly matters; and it will need to do so in the context of the religious and ideological pluralism of our society. This is the setting of the grace—full witness of Christians to Jesus Christ. The ministry of pastoral care, then, finds its identity, its purpose and ultimately its resources as part of the fulfilment of the Christian mission, which in turn finds its identity in the mission of God Himself whose intention is that 'I will be their God, and they will be my people' (Revelation 21.7). It is into this covenant community, engaged in mission, that Christian believers are baptized (Ephesians 4.1-6).

3. Pastoral Care finds its true focus in Worship

The spiritual, practical and theological life of the Christian community comes into sharp focus when the community of the baptised worship together. The way worship and liturgy are conducted and owned by the local Christian community speaks volumes for the spiritual and pastoral integrity of that community. In the absence of a centralized teaching authority such as that of the Roman Catholic Church, the faith of the Church of England finds its clearest expression in its written and celebrated liturgies and in its public prayer and hymnody. It is within the spaciousness and embodiment of the worshipping community that believers find themselves received, accepted, challenged, affirmed, loved, and their communal and personal vocation renewed. Robin Green[56] has written evocatively of 'worship that cares for us'. This is worship that because it is genuinely and authentically offered to the God who cares, expresses (embodies) the concern for the person of the God who cares.

One of the key needs Anglicans have who participate in public worship is the need for a genuineness about the forgiveness of their sins, and the affirmation through reconciliation of their continuing part in the community of faith. This is offered formally within the liturgy through the General Confession, the Peace and the Agnus Dei. Liturgical leadership that is sensitive to 'the silent music of the congregation', preaching that deals with reality, and prayer that arises out of the community that serves Christ all have key parts to play. The ministry of pastoral care is not in a different department from the ministry of public worship—if that happens pastoral care loses its identity and purpose and worship loses its theological integrity. That is, pastoral care and worship share the same eschatological agenda of the covenant community engaged in mission. Among the principal purposes of public worship are that it should be *the* embodiment of God's care for his people; the embodied offering of their service in adoration, prayer and commitment, and the embodiment of their renewal as the community of the baptised sent forth in the mission of the Gospel.

Pastoral Importance of Reconciliation Rites

Each of the different components of public liturgy need to find their expression in the personal ministry of pastoral care—preparation and welcome, penitence,

---

56   Robin Green, *Only Connect : Worship and Liturgy from the Perspective of Pastoral Care* (DLT, London, 1987).

ministry of the word, intercession and thanksgiving, the sharing of peace, eucharist, renewal of commitment, sending forth. Among these, penitence has found a very muted expression among Anglicans. Many find the perfunctory and unimaginative way in which the General Confession is often handled unhelpful. Although the availability of personal ministry for those 'who by this means cannot quiet his own conscience herein, but requireth further comfort or counsel,'[57] is increasingly well known and resorted to, the absence of authorized rites for the reconciliation of penitents has been a very serious liturgical, pastoral and mission deficiency in our church.

When we look wider, to those times when the community may need to recognise and welcome the penitence of a person who has become publicly estranged from them, or where the community as a whole needs to express its grief over the sin of the church or the sinfulness of our world, the current absence of appropriate rites *that are the common currency of the believing community,* amounts to a positive deprivation. That means in turn that this absence is likely to serve in some sense as an inhibitor in the effectiveness of the local church engaged in mission.

The recent secularization of pastoral care into some kinds of counselling, and even some kinds of 'presence ministry', serves to privatise the church's care and thus restrict the church's mission. The Rites of Reconciliation point decisively in the direction of the community facing spiritual and vocational realities among its membership, precisely because the reconciliation being sought and offered is the reconciliation of the baptized. It may be argued that the rites may be highly valued by the ordained leadership of the Church, but are likely to be rarely used by the mainstream community. This may be true, but I would argue that the very *presence* of such rites in the Church of England's liturgical provision will have a teaching and pastoral role of great importance in fostering our vocation to engage in the mission of reconciliation of the world with Jesus Christ.

One of the arguments that has been deployed against the inclusion of the Rites of Reconciliation in the liturgical provision of the Church of England concerns a worry about giving too much emphasis to the place of sin in relation to confession, and to the priest as the agent of absolution. The reasons for this are many and include an in-built suspicion among evangelicals of ritual of any sort, and a sense of having to be loyal to the Reformation move away from the role of priest as intermediary. It is vital however that we allow ourselves to grow from our history rather than be prisoners of it. As we have seen, engaging in personal and community ritualization is an inescapable part of being human and living together. The only choice we have is what sort of ritualization we engage in and how we formulate out public rituals so that they are the best possible expression of our intention—in this case in relation to penitence.

At the centre of every rite of reconciliation is the act of speaking our confession and of hearing the word of absolution. The theology of this needs to be understood

---

in the most direct possible way so that the rite can enable the greatest possible liveliness of engagement. In the New Testament owning up to one's sinful deeds is only one usage of the verb 'to confess' (*homologeo*). Much more often it is used to establish a sense of relationship, of belonging together. We can put it like this: the primary Christian confession is not 'I've done this, that or the other and am very sorry'; but 'Jesus Christ is Lord' (Romans 10. 9-10). The act of confession within the Rite of Reconciliation is all about the penitent confessing Jesus as Lord, and therefore their own unworthiness and need for forgiveness, healing, renewal. In this context the words of absolution are much more a prayer for the return and renewal of the Holy Spirit, than a mere (?) lifting of a burden. The penitent and the reconciling community together are seeking for spiritual renewal, integrity, and grace to live the mission of the baptized in the world. The proposed rites, with their essential form of welcoming, clarifying roles (so that the penitent can be a penitent), the sharing of scripture, space for confession and counsel, the prayers of forgiveness and of blessing, give clear shape to the kind of pastoral care we have been discussing.

5
Absolution Reconsidered
by Gordon Jeanes

'The difference that is between the priest and the layman in [the eucharist] is only in the ministration; that the priest, as a common minister of the church, doth minister and distribute the Lord's supper unto other, and other receive it at his hands . . . And this nothing diminisheth the estimation and dignity of priesthood and other ministers of the church, but advanceth and highly commendeth their ministration. For if they are much to be loved, honoured and esteemed, that be the kings, chancellors, judges, officers, and ministers in temporal matters; how much then are they to be esteemed, that be ministers of Christ's words and sacraments, and have to them committed the keys of heaven, to let in and shut out by the ministration of his word and gospel?'[58]

When we examine declarations of absolution, we are confronted with an important issue in the theology of ministry: how do we speak authoritatively of God's will or action in a particular situation? This issue raises questions both about the theology of what we are doing and about the language we use. Broadly speaking, we have to sail between the Scylla of too easily identifying God's way with our own, and the Charybdis of being reduced to agnostic silence. The issue raises itself in various ways for all Christians in every walk of life. Here we are considering simply one particular instance, of sinners seeking God's mercy and looking for a declaration of his forgiveness. Since I am concentrating on the actual words of absolution, I lay aside other issues such as the minister of reconciliation, scripture and ecclesiological questions.

For Anglicans the starting point of this liturgical question is usually the Book of Common Prayer and the Articles, Canons and Homilies. In the Communion Service, the first Exhortation invites people to examine their lives and come to the Table in repentance and trust in God's mercy. And the priest tells them,

'And because it is requisite that no man should come to the Holy Communion, but with a full trust in God's mercy, and with a quiet conscience; therefore if there be any of you, who by this means cannot quiet his own conscience herein, but requireth further comfort or counsel, let him come to me, or to some other discreet and learned Minister of God's Word, and open his grief; that by the ministry of God's holy Word he may receive the benefit of absolution, together with ghostly counsel and advice, to the quieting of his conscience, and avoiding of all scruple and doubtfulness.'

The practice advocated here is clearly meant to be optional, and we are not told if there is any particular structure the encounter is meant to have. The description given here suggests a somewhat informal structure, adjusted to the pastoral needs of each situation. And as we read further in the Book of Common Prayer and take

---

58 Cranmer on the position of clergy: *Defence* 5.11. P.S., 350

41

into account the successive editions of the Book we see that this is indeed the case. While there was a difference of wording in this exhortation between the 1662 edition and its predecessors going back to the Second Prayer Book of Edward VI (1552), the First Prayer Book of 1549 spells out more fully the optional nature of recourse to a priest, telling those who use 'the auricular and secret confession to the priest' and those who 'shall be satisfied with a general confession' not to be offended by one another. And in the Visitation of the Sick there is in all the editions provision for optional 'special confession'. In 1549, a form of absolution follows, with the rubric stating, 'After which confession, the priest shall absolve him after this form: and the same form of absolution shall be used in all private confessions'. In 1552 the reference to other private confessions is removed, and in 1662 the form of absolution is itself made an option following the optional confession. Since this is the only direction given for the structure and content of quieting the individual conscience, it is clearly left open to the discretion of the minister and the individual. By 1662 the latter has considerable control of the situation.

It would seem at first sight that the aim of the successive revisions was solely to diminish the role and function of individual confession. However the reformers saw their aim being rather to restore a godly practice to its original state. What they disagreed with was the medieval requirement laid down in the Lateran Council of 1215 that all adults must make particular confession of all their sins to their own priest before making communion, which had to be received at least every Easter. Against this the Anglican reformers proposed an optional pastoral rite. Much of their rhetoric was focussed negatively against the medieval practice, and even the Homily of Repentance, written early in Elizabeth's reign, attacks the old pattern as much as it proposes the new. In effect it compares the Anglican ministry with the traditional auricular confession in an early version of the formula, 'All can, none must':

> 'I do not say but that, if any do find themselves troubled in conscience, they may repair to their learned curate or pastor, or to some other godly learned man, and shew the trouble and doubt of their conscience to them, that they may receive at their hand the comfortable salve of God's word: but it is against the true Christian's liberty, that any man should be bound to the numbering of his sins, as it hath been used heretofore in the time of blindness and ignorance.'[59]

So it was not the intention of the reformers simply to scrap confession and leave nothing in its place. The medieval office is replaced by a ministry which is, at least in the way it is described in formularies and other contemporary accounts, more pastorally based. The Anglican version, based on true Christian liberty, provides a pastoral response in an optional, not obligatory, rite.

Canon 113 of the Canons of 1604 deals specifically with this situation in stipulating that:

> 'If any man confess his secret and hidden sins to the Minister, for the unburdening of his conscience, and to receive spiritual consolation and

---

59   Homily of Repentance (Second Part), p 577.

ease of mind from him; we . . . do strictly charge and admonish him, that he do not at any time reveal and make known to any person whatsoever any crime or offence so committed to his trust and secrecy.' How was such a ministry exercised? The Prayer Book sets out the same pastoral model: one who wishes to take advantage of the ministry approaches some 'discreet and learned minister of God's word', and receives counsel and advice and 'by the ministry of God's word he may receive comfort and the benefit of absolution.'[60]

In fact the reformers were keen to promote their own form of ecclesiastical discipline which would keep open evil livers from the communion table, and would submit them to excommunication and public penance. In the Prayer Book we find only the wish for this expressed in the Commination Service, but there was detailed provision in a draft revised Canon Law Code, known today as the *Reformatio Legum*. This was the unfinished side of Cranmer's reformation of the Church of England.

So as we approach the Reformation material, we have to set aside the negative polemic against the medieval system and take seriously the positive programme of public confession of sins in regular church worship, an optional pastoral rite of confession of sins in which the form and content is left to the needs of the penitent and the discretion of the minister, particular provision for ministry of the sick, and the provision of excommunication, public penance and restoration to communion. How did Cranmer and his colleagues express God's forgiving love in these pastoral encounters?

Cranmer understood worship and the sacraments as signs of God's promises of grace. The notion of a sacrament as 'the outward and visible sign of an inward and spiritual grace' is worked systematically into the liturgy, especially in 1552, where in the Communion Service the priest prays that 'we receiving . . . this bread and wine . . . may be partakers of his most blessed Body and Blood'. In other words: all the communicants receive the bread and wine. It is by God's grace that they receive the Body and Blood of Christ, but the faithful do so in the confidence that they are obeying Christ's command and trusting in his promise of grace. Brian Gerrish has described this understanding of the sacraments as 'symbolic parallelism'. The human and the divine actions are distinct. The freedom of God's action is respected by the distinction, but his promise to act is perceived by the faith of the recipient as the connection between the two actions. The approach pervades all of Cranmer's liturgical writing, and has seeped into the later history of Anglican worship, for example with the common petition for the consecration of the bread and wine in the Eucharist, that they 'may be to us the Body and Blood' of Christ. This, based on 1549, leaves open the exact relation of the sign to the signified, whether one is encompassed in the other, and thereby embraces the spectrum of Anglican theology. But the spectrum itself is based on the notion of outward sign and inward grace.

---

60   Exhortation before Communion. The wording of 1552 and 1662 varies but not significantly.

This is what we see in the various forms of absolution in the Prayer Book. Each one carefully avoids speaking without qualification for the divine action. In the Communion Service the operative words, 'have mercy upon you, pardon and deliver you from all your sins' etc. are expressed in the subjunctive, and they are qualified by the introductory clause, that God has promised forgiveness to 'all them that with hearty repentance and true faith turn unto him'. The absolution in Morning and Evening Prayer is even more convoluted, with a declaration of God's forgiveness of all who 'truly repent and unfeignedly believe his holy Gospel', followed by a prayer for that repentance, so that the congregation is left wondering whether they have heard an actual declaration of forgiveness of their sins or a general description of God's policy towards sinful humanity.

Now we must turn to the formula which, in later history, has been the most tendentious, that of the absolution in the Visitation of the Sick.

'Our Lord Jesus Christ, who hath left power to his Church to absolve all sinners who truly repent and believe in him, of his great mercy forgive thee thine offences: And by his authority committed to me, I absolve thee from all thy sins, in the name of the Father and of the Son, and of the Holy Ghost. Amen.'

Some have seen this prayer as the vehicle of priestly arrogance or, less wickedly, as a fossil of medieval devotion. But in fact it has undergone the same qualifications as the other formulae. First, there is the clause which tells us that this will apply only to those who have true repentance and faith. Then there is a distinction between God's action (here, explicitly, to forgive) and that of the Church and the minister (who absolve). The absolution is the sign of God's forgiveness.[61]

The draft *Reformatio Legum* took the same approach. There is a long and full rite for the reconciliation of an excommunicate person. The pastor meets the penitent outside the church door. The penitent declares his willingness to repent and his desire to be reintegrated, and is brought by the pastor into the church. Then follows a very long exhortation and a confession by the penitent, first as a prayer to God and then in an address to the congregation, in which he names his offence. The pastor asks the congregation if they are willing to forgive and receive him. He addresses the penitent who is kneeling, then,

'*Here the pastor, touching the head of the accused, shall continue as follows:* Before this church, the government of which has been entrusted to me, I absolve you *(ego te exsolvo)* of the penalty of your transgressions and release you from the bonds of excommunication, by the authority of God, the power of Jesus Christ and the Holy Spirit, with the agreement of all the

---

61 This analysis is corroborated when we look at Cranmer's likely sources, the Sarum rite and that of Archbishop Hermann of Cologne (Brightman, *English Rite* p 828). Here we see the insertion of the qualifying clause into the Sarum rite, and also that it is Cranmer's initiative to distinguish between 'forgive' and 'absolve' while Sarum and Hermann use the same word, 'absolve' without distinction. (S) Dominus noster iesus christus **(H) hanc Ecclesiae suae potestatem reliquit, ut eos a peccatis absolvat . . . quicunque peccatorum poenitentes Christo Domino vere credunt** pro sua magna pietate te absolvat: et ego auctoritate eiusdem dei domini nostri iesu christi . . . et auctoritate mihi tradita absolvo te ab omnibus peccatis . . . tuis . . . In nomine patris et filii et spiritus sancti. Amen.

members of this church here present and also with the assent of the bishop, and I restore you to your former place and full rights in the church.'[62] Then the pastor embraces and kisses the penitent, takes him by the hand and leads him to a place by the Table for the Holy Communion while the Te Deum or Gloria in Excelsis is sung. There follow a versicle and response, a prayer of thanksgiving and an exhortation to the penitent against repeating his crime.

The important bit here is the prayer of absolution. The 'ego te' form is retained without apology. The word 'exsolvo' is a bit odd. A glance at the dictionary underlines my gut suspicion that it is the same as 'absolvo' but simply lacks the traditional ecclesiastical overtones. We may suppose therefore that here the distinction between divine and human, sign and signified, has been abandoned. However earlier in the exhortation the pastor says to the penitent:

'Therefore you must diligently investigate all things, to ensure that you do not wickedly abuse the dignity of my office in order to deceive God and the Holy Spirit. For it is certain, my brother, that however we poor men are tossed about, God will not be mocked. Therefore watch out again and again, lest you do something in this most holy business by craft or deceit. We are the external witnesses of your submission, which we have observed, but God enters into the secret and totally hidden recesses of your mind, and is most deeply offended if he finds any trace of perfidy in you.'[63]

This paragraph must stand as the important qualifier on everything that is conducted. 'We are the external witnesses.'[64]

What do we discover from this survey of the Reformation material? First, that Cranmer and his colleagues had a clear positive picture of the exercise and discipline of penitence, different from the medieval system, and which they believed to be a restoration of the authentic approach of the first Christians: of penitence and forgiveness expressed in the general confession and absolution provided by the public liturgy, of the optional pastoral ministry with particular emphasis on times of sickness, and the provision (never enacted) of

---

62 *Reformatio Legum* 33: *Formula reconciliationis excommunicatorum;* in G Bray (ed.), *Tudor Church Reform: the Henrician Canons of 1535 and the Reformatio Legum Ecclesiasticarum* (Church of England Record Society, Boydell Press, 2000) p 489.

63 *Ibid.,* p.483.

64 Cf. Cranmer, *Defence* V.3 (Parker Society, pp 347-8)
[The Old Testament fathers used sacrifices] 'as certain ceremonies, whereby such persons as had offended against the law of Moses, and were cast out of the congregation, were received again among the people, and declared to be absolved. As for like purposes we use in the church of Christ sacraments by him instituted. And this outward casting out from the people of God, and receiving in again was according to the law and knowledge of man; but the true reconciliation and forgiveness of sin before God neither the fathers of the old law had, nor we yet have, but only by the sacrifice of Christ.'
This use of 'witness' language need not be limited to a 'low' theology of the minister of absolution, as we see from the Slavonic Orthodox tradition described by Kallistos Ware (*The Orthodox Church* (Pelican, 1972), p 296)
'Behold, my child, Christ stands here invisibly and receives your confession. Therefore do not be ashamed nor afraid; conceal nothing from me, but tell me without hesitation everything that you have done, and so you shall have pardon from Our Lord Jesus Christ. See, his holy icon is before us: and I am a witness, bearing testimony before him of all the things which you have to say to me. But if you conceal anything from me, you shall have the greater sin. Take heed, therefore, lest having come to a physician you depart unhealed'.

excommunication and public reconciliation of notorious sinners. Along with this scheme there is a confident language of the primacy of God's grace which stands free and sovereign over all human endeavour, and under God the clergy, as ministers of the Church, 'have to them committed the keys of heaven, to let in and shut out by the ministration of his word and gospel'. The issue here is not how high or low one's theology is of Church or ministry, but of respecting the right order and relation. First God, then the Church, then the authorised ministers of the Church. In the words of John Robinson, you can have as high a theology of the ministry as you like, as long as you have a higher theology of the Church. And likewise you can have as high a theology of the Church as you like, as long as you have a higher theology of the Gospel and Kingdom of God.

Such was Cranmer's scheme of penitential discipline (of which only a small part was ever enacted) and his pattern of proposing the way in which the minister speaks of God's forgiveness. The Reformation system was practised in subsequent generations, we cannot tell to what extent or in what ways. But references and discussions show that it was by no means unknown. We must now turn our gaze to the nineteenth century when the practice of confession and absolution, which seems to have become much reduced, was vigorously revived under the Oxford Movement and became a matter of controversy. It is very difficult to find a balanced discussion of the debates of the time. Much writing even in our own generation takes up polemical positions, so that, depending on whom you are reading, you cannot imagine who could possibly support private confession or, alternatively, who in their right mind would ever oppose it. The most interesting discussion I have been able to find is John Kent's Holding the Fort in which he portrays confession as akin to revivalist evangelical conversion—a moment of heartfelt conviction and repentance. There was a difference as well, as Kent points out: confession was an ongoing activity: ' "Conversion" formed part of the evangelical's past; confession remained integral to the anglo-catholic's future.' There were other issues as well: Kent portrays the advocacy of confession as part of the clergy's assertion of the authority of the Church (and the status of the clergy) over against the rise of science and the new professions. In this they failed: the laity did not vest their confidence in the priest's advice in matters of personal conduct.[65] But the anglo-catholic programme left a deep distrust among other Anglicans of the discipline of confession and absolution, with accusations of tyranny on the part of the priest, psychological dependency on the part of the penitent and so on, and largely focussed on the absolution formula with its statement, 'I absolve you'. Cranmer's attempt to maintain but strictly to qualify the minister's role had now backfired.

Kent's examination of the nineteenth century is very important. He distinguishes between two issues. The attempt of the anglo-catholic clergy to bolster the status of the Church through confession failed and is now history. The power of individual confession lay in the penitent's experience of ongoing

---

67 *Holding the Fort: Studies in Victorian Revivalism* (Epworth, London, 1978). There is also a useful discussion of this period by Nigel Yates, 'Jesuits in Disguise? Ritualist Confessors and their Critics in the 1870s', in *Journal of Ecclesiastical History*, 39, (1988), 202-216.

conversion and commitment. The penitent may not have exercised such autonomy over the details as was proposed in the 1662 Prayer Book, but was still the person who owned the situation most fully.

What are we to do now in the light of this history?

We have ended up in a situation where, in the Church of England, some people are vehemently opposed to the particular formula of absolution with the words, 'I absolve you'. At the same time there are those members of the Church of England for whom these same words are all important. It is the penitent who is most wedded to them; the words focus the entire engagement.

In liturgical revision this clash must be acknowledged and both sides taken seriously. Few theologians, if any, would hold that the words are theologically necessary in the rite; but as 'associational language' they have a validity, indeed there should be a strong presumption for their inclusion; we also need to take into account the theological criticisms made against the formula. Proposed reforms of the formula would seek to preserve the controverted words by setting them in a context that protects them, as far as possible, from misunderstanding and abuse. In effect the procedure is no different from other cases (e.g. different renderings of the institution narrative in the eucharistic prayer) where words of great associational importance to say the least are made available to the worshipper of every tradition by a careful rendering of their context according to the theological and liturgical norms of each tradition.

Criticisms of the Prayer Book formula might point to the heavy emphasis on the power and authority of Church and priest, which speaks heavily of the sixteenth century. The absence of a theology of the Holy Spirit is typical of Cranmer but would be lamented today. In any event the formula would be found wanting: it suggests more that the Church long ago replaced Christ in an administrative function than that it is acting in the presence of his Spirit, and that the role of the priest is not well integrated with the divine action.

The Roman Catholic post-Tridentine formula[66] is close to that of the traditional Anglican formula and suffers from the same problem. A proposed reform of this formula after the Second Vatican Council is discussed by Bugnini.[67] If I read Bugnini correctly, the Congregation for Divine Worship proposed that the prayer of absolution be amended so that God is the subject of all the performative verbs and the phrase under question should read 'and *therefore* absolve'. This was rejected by the Congregation for the Doctrine of the Faith who want, 'and *I* absolve you'. According to Bugnini, there was widespread support from the *periti* for the first option: 'it sought to bring out the fact that God forgives through Jesus Christ, who in turn acts in his Church. "And I", on the other hand, makes a

---

66 ROMAN RITUAL 1839 (Dudley and Rowell p 184)
    Dominus noster Jesus Christus te absolvat, et ego auctoritate ipsius te absolvo ab omni vinculo excommunicationis, suspensionis et interdicti, in quantum possum et tu indiges: deinde, Ego te absolvo a peccatis tuis; in nomine Patris et Filii + et Spiritus sancti. Amen.
    May our Lord Jesus Christ absolve you, and by his authority I absolve you from every bond of excommunication, suspension and interdict insofar as I am able and you require: then, I absolve you from your sins, in the name of the Father and of the Son and of the Holy Spirit. Amen.
67 *Reform of the Liturgy 1948-1975*, p 674.

distinction between two subjects, "God and I", so that the priest's act seems to be as it were added on to the first part of the formula rather than intrinsically connected with it.' But the Congregation for the Doctrine of the Faith rejected it without revealing their reasons.

The moral is that if 'I absolve you' in the absolution form is to be commended to the Church of England then it must be clearly and appropriately linked to the divine action, and that today would be seen as being within the life and power of the Holy Spirit given by the risen Christ for the forgiveness of sins in the grace of baptism which operates throughout our lives. In summary, a formula of absolution would include the following features.

1. An emphasis on the Holy Spirit in the prayer for forgiveness, in addition to or instead of the 'power and authority' emphasis of the present formula.
2. A ministerial declaration of forgiveness in the form of the traditional performative text: 'I absolve you'.
3. A clear dynamic relationship between the two elements, preserving the priority of the divine action and the intimate relation of the ministerial declaration.

In accordance with the above discussion we offer the following draft for the absolution formula:

> Our Lord Jesus Christ,
> who in the power of his resurrection
> entrusts the Spirit of reconciliation to his church
> forgive you and free you from the bonds of sin;
> as a sign and witness of his redeeming love,
> I absolve you from all your sins,
> in the name of the Father, and of the Son, and of the Holy Spirit. **Amen.**

The starting point is the 1662 formula of absolution in the Visitation of the Sick which is used for its importance as associational language—it has significance by its very familiarity.

The draft seeks:

1. to begin with Christ and to state that forgiveness of sins is by the power of the resurrection. Everything else derives from that.
2. to emphasize the role and guidance of Holy Spirit in the ministry of reconcilation
3. to make it clear that Christ himself is the one who forgives sin.
4. to make clear the role of the priest as the one who absolves i.e. declares Christ's forgiveness. By the authority of the Church and in the discernment of the Spirit the priest proclaims God's redeeming work, but it is God's work. Hence the priest is described as sign and witness. This is a common theme in the traditions of both East and West and seeks to avoid only the misunderstandings of the minister's role as being over priest-centred or over-juridical.